Getting Ready for Love

LOVING GOD. LOVING ME. LOVING YOU.

By
L. Spenser Smith

WITH SPECIAL INSIGHTS FROM
Gwendolyn Y. Townsend

PRESS

Copyright © 2009 by L. Spenser Smith

Getting Ready for Love
Loving God. Loving Me. Loving You.
by L. Spenser Smith

Printed in the United States of America

ISBN 978-1-60791-863-9

L. Spenser Smith Ministries
P.O. Box 41009
Tuscaloosa, Alabama 35404
(205) 554-0657
www.lspensersmith.org
www.theblessedofbothworlds.com

www.xulonpress.com

••• TABLE OF CONTENTS •••

••• ACKNOWLEDGEMENTS •••

To My Heavenly Father who loves me more than I ever thought I deserved. My life is yours to use as long as I live.

To my beautiful vessel of love and understanding, my wife, Patrice: When I first saw you that night in Foster Tanner Music Building at choir rehearsal, I didn't know where our journey would take us. I thank you for being patient and loving even in the times when I was not *ready for love*. The love you have given me has strengthened my courage and covered me on my quest fulfill my life's assignment. I pray that I have brought as much joy and happiness as you have brought to me. I am privileged to call you my wife. 4/25/72 is the day an angel was born!

To my children, Jori, Jamel, and Jarren. To see you live and grow is a clear indication that God loves me. I pray that you will live by the lesson that "TeeTee" Gwen and I have written, as this book becomes a shining guide preparing you to discover the loves of your lives. Daddy, loves his "Js"!!

To my parents Joseph and Lynette. You raised me to be the best I could be. Your unconditional love got me through some of the most awkward years of my life. You mean the world to me. I thank God everyday for you. To my second mother, Beverly Moore. You literally have taught me about lasting love and perseverance. When problems blind me, I see the vision coming to pass in your eyes. Thank you for your strength.

To my siblings, Ty & Shell, Curt & Shani, John & Danielle. Let's continue to teach a new generation how to love.

Getting Ready for Love
A Special Dedication

● ● ●

This book is dedicated to my dear sister, Gwendolyn Townsend who passed away in January 2003. She was more than just my sister; she was one of my best and dearest friends.

Following my sister's death, one of the workers at the church where Gwen served as administrator, located some invaluable files on her computer. Among the collection was a book she was writing called *Getting Ready for Love: When You've Loved and Lost*. It was something I knew she was working on because we often talked about love, relationships, and intimacy; why women are so hurt and why men are so foolish (at least in her mind). To receive the incomplete manuscript was worth more to me than any monetary inheritance she could have left.

As I began to read it, I saw the pain of her experiences and the wisdom she learned from them as she spoke very candidly to women about the do's and don'ts of being a single woman in pursuit of living Godly while desiring intimate fulfillment. I was literally amazed at how she communicated her heart so vividly, even at the risk of exposing herself to the judgmental gazes of others. She was intelligent, articulate and humorous. Gwen possessed a prevailing anointing that she wove into a powerful message for women so that they could avoid the hidden pitfalls of flawed relationships, heal from the pain of their pasts, and be optimistically hopeful about their futures-whether married or single. She was not afraid to be transparent. What a woman!

My sister knew love but love never knew her. It sometimes only wanted to express itself to her in the shadows but never really celebrate her in the light of day, thus depriving her of an urgent need to feel significant. I often wondered how she could bring fulfillment to the lives of others and yet be so void and empty within herself.

When I decided to write a book about love and relationships, I remembered her manuscript. God had given me some insight into the subject matter and as a man and pastor who has given counsel to so many in this area, a book of this kind was needed. I thought, however, it was more than fitting for her to share in the writing of this book. I adopted her original title and used what God had given me as the subtext. Some passages from her manuscript have been extracted because I believe they are simply too personal and painful to share. Prayerfully, I included portions that although they were originally written to women, they would bless the lives of men as well. They are clearly designated as *"Words to the Ladies from Gwen."*

For the years that she spoke volumes of courage to me, I owe her my voice and in this book, I graciously lend it to her to share and speak some of her last statements of wit, insight and wisdom to the world. Get ready to love. I love you, sis.

Gwendolyn Yvonne Townsend
1965-2003

First Encounters with the Love

● ● ●

*"When I was a child, I spoke as a child, I under-
stood as a child, I thought as a child..."*
(I Corinthians 13:11)

Everyone has a personal story of how they have arrived
at their definition of love. For some, the journey was
filled the techni-color of a brilliant romance and courtship
often read about in novels or seen in the movies; demonstrated by hand holding, eye-gazing, and warm kisses laced
with promises for the future.

Then there are others who have come to know love in
black and white mixed with a whole lot of gray; "trape-
zing" from one sweeping moment of passion to the tears of
a broken and betrayed heart, swinging from relationship to
relationship with the hopes of never falling to their death.

Yes, we all have our journeys that represent our first
encounters with love. Each journey has worked to build the
integral foundation of our personal definition of what love
is, should be like, and what our role is in its unfolding. Our
personal definitions are the key components of our personal
decisions. In short, how we decide to love and allow ourselves
to be loved is based upon what it has come to mean to each
of us- a meaning that is taught and based sometimes more
upon our environment than our own experience.

Learning Love at a Young Age

My first "mentally recordable" experience with love occurred when I was about 10 years old. My life of climbing trees and riding bikes was abruptly interrupted with these strange "feelings" I had for this young girl. She lived across the field from my uncle's house. She had a beautiful smile and was extremely shy. The first time I saw her, I was immediately smitten like Alfalfa's first glance at Darla (I'm a Little Rascals fan). I don't know what it was but there was something special about her, even at that age. I wanted to protect her from other little boys on the playground. I wanted to do her homework. I wanted to sit by her at lunch. I wanted to marry her! (Yes at 10 years old!).

Over time we became good friends and when I turned 13, I planned to make it official! Then something happened. I noticed that the more I tried to get her to notice me, the more she was attracted to other guys. Thug ragamuffins!! She was interested in guys who could have been candidates for juvenile detention. There I was, a straight A student with my heart in my hand, loving someone who didn't return it the way I gave it.

Don't get me wrong; I did have other little girlfriends to supposedly preoccupy my time. I would hold their hands in front of her to see if she would get jealous. She was, but never reciprocated any genuine feelings for me.

Then on Valentine's Day, all of my feelings were shattered when she started to seriously date another guy. Everybody knew about it; everybody except me. I had picked the perfect Valentine's card for her and was just about to give it, when I witnessed the ultimate betrayal. Without her ever noticing I was there, I saw that she was in a real relationship with someone else. To add insult to injury, he had a gold tooth!! I was hurt with seemingly no one to talk to. All my friends knew and no one ever told me. I made the biggest fool of myself. How could she do this to me? I didn't have enough sense to know then what I know now. Simply put, you can't make somebody love you.

As time went on and I matured, I discovered that nothing I did for her would have made a difference in how she felt about me. She didn't use me. She later admitted that she didn't respond to my affection because she didn't realize how special she was and did not believe she deserved love in that way. Her life's experiences gave her many reasons why she was not worthy. After hearing her explanation, I began to investigate love a little deeper.

How could anyone refuse genuine love simply because they did not feel worthy? In addition, how could you give something to someone that you've never experienced for yourself? Why would God put love in the earth and then let it sometimes hurt so badly? What are we missing?

I Still "Love" Love

After all that I have experienced thus far in my life, I can honestly say that love, as it has been negatively viewed by so many, has never been my enemy. I grew up seeing love's joys and pains. I saw love help forgive some of the most hurtful transgressions of the heart. I have seen love celebrate at weddings and cry at funerals. I *love* love.

Even though I remain on a quest to understand it, love has never failed me. It has taken some time to see it, but I have come to this conclusion all the same. Love treats us according to our knowledge of how it functions. This is why this book is so important.

Many people have approached love simply from varying gender perspectives. Men do this. Women do that. While those points of view are all relevant, I dare to take a different approach; to reveal that love can only work to its maximum benefit when it is done IN ORDER.

Reader, this book is your tool for learning about the commonalities we all share while in pursuit of finding love.

As I honestly share my heart and my journey to knowing who and what love is, I urge you to get ready for love!

The Order of Love

I charge you…. Do not stir up nor awaken love
until it pleases
(Song of Solomon 8:4)

Let all things be done decently and in order.
(I Corinthians 14:40)

Because love is mostly thought to be an emotion or feeling, very seldom do we realize that it should be approached and engaged with a degree of order and priority. All of us have been victims of the "love just happening" syndrome. Because love is vitally important to who we are, it deserves our earnest consideration in how we prepare to give our hearts and express this most important ideal.

Real love emanates blessing and favor. It is constructed and released to allow us to experience happiness and endure pain. Within love, we find life's most certain fulfillments along with its definite challenges. It can be the source of our greatest highs and our deepest lows. It moves us to tears and gives us "god-like" bursts of strength that enable us to protect what we deem as precious. Yet as important as love is, this concept is highly misunderstood. What a tragedy! But take heart! When love is properly defined, understood and in order, we can live in a place of complete wholeness and absolute happiness.

Ignorance is Not Bliss

"Ignorance is not bliss; especially when what you don't know is the only thing that can bless you."

The origin of our definition of love is rarely from the perspective of the divine. God is love. To erroneously define love is to erroneously define God. Our warped definition of this powerful word often leads to the misunderstandings and misgivings found within relationships. Men are afraid to say it. Women are waiting to hear it. And in between, we are ruining our lives.

As men, we are subtly taught to never mention the word. It's an irreversible "trap" that if ever said to a woman, will cause us a world of pain and agony. We fear that <u>love</u> being sandwiched between two principled pronouns, namely "I" and "you" causes irrevocable damage to our world of masculine freedom.

For women, love is something they willingly give, even when it is not returned. A woman dreams of being whisked away in the arms of the perfect man who showers and pampers her with love and affection Unfortunately in many cases, this woman eventually finds herself disillusioned because she has unwittingly made the wrong man her priority, while in contrast, he simply made her one of his options.

Misconceptions of what it takes to love purely and optimally are the primary reasons why so many walk away from love on every level. Many people are highly skeptical, asking if true love really exists, and if it does, will it ever find them. I believe it will, but it may take some time. To find it, we must eliminate our own selfish eagerness to be "in love" and seek the proper order of how to love, when to love, and who qualifies for our love. When we follow these steps, we will be well on our way into developing lasting covenantal relationships.

In the Song of Solomon, the Shulamite woman charges her companion to not stir up love until it comes of its own accord. These are wise words that can be applied to us today. When we became saved, we immediately began to learn the principles of the Kingdom. We began to replace much of what we'd learned in the kingdom of darkness with truth from the kingdom of light. Unfortunately tragedy comes when we are not taught kingdom principles in specific areas of our lives. When we are ignorant to new and vital principles for life where pertinent information is required in order to make critical decisions, we rely on what we've either previously heard or experienced.

No one really tells us how to navigate through love and relationships once we get saved. The answer is simple; love really shouldn't be that hard. Love should be easy, and yet it can be one of the most difficult things to properly experience in your life. Regrettably, most of us bring our previous concepts of dating, courtship, singleness, and marriage into our life with the Lord. This is one area where it doesn't occur to us to change our mentality because in actuality, no one really expects us to. We are comfortable making our own "patchwork theology; borrowing from "this" teaching and "that" ministry and "those" relatives and relationships. Because we are rarely taught about love and relationships within the Body of Christ, anointed, saved, and single men and women bear the scars of rejection, disappointment, anger, fear, hurt and pain all in the name of love. We must deal with those things that we have consciously or unconsciously done that put our hearts in jeopardy. We can no longer **practice love without a license**. It damages our lives and the lives of others. It creates a poor witness for God and misrepresents the Kingdom throughout the world.

The Shulamite's words readily relay that there is a right time for love. It will come when it is ready. It will not be forced. Love is one of life's great risks and it requires all who desire it to be prepared for it BEFORE it shows up. This applies to both saved and unsaved, sinner and saint.

All of us have experienced the embarrassment and pain of unreciprocated love simply because we did not know and were not taught that love works best when we are prepared for it when it comes. Diana Ross and the Supremes said it best:

I need love, love
To ease my mind
I need to find, find someone to call mine
But mama said

You can't hurry love
No, you just have to wait
She said love don't come easy
It's a game of give and take

You can't hurry love
No, you just have to wait
You got to trust, give it time
No matter how long it takes

In our eagerness to experience love, we seldom evaluate ourselves to see if we are ready to love, be loved, and to be in love. I can honestly admit that at one time, I was as ill equipped to love as a man with no feet with a closet full of shoes. My desire, even as a child, to love and experience that love from someone else, led me to do things that were both hurtful and confusing. I gave up my virginity before time and because I wanted to be accepted, I was easily manipulated into giving up other precious things that made me unique. I risked not pleasing God because I wanted to have someone by my side. I don't fault anyone for my failures; I simply admit that I practiced love without a license. In honest reflection, I am confident that we all have found ourselves in this position at least once.

We want love, but don't know how to properly manage it. It took me years to discover that love had an order attached to it. That revelation was birthed at a time when I knew I had allowed my ignorance of how love worked to back me into a corner leaving me completely broken and confused. I felt that love had led me down the wrong street and left me stranded in the dark alley of loneliness and embarrassment. During that low time, God revealed that true love has an order and if I would follow it, I would be rewarded with love's full benefits.

The Order of Love

With God, order is everything. In the beginning, God established His order before He released His image. He first set the patterns, borders and parameters of every facet of the Garden of Eden, and then He released His image, man and woman, into it. We often ignore this fact. The maximum benefit of all that God has created for us to enjoy is realized when we are in the right order. Order has a way of making God's original intent clearer and readily accessible. However, when we do not pursue order, we stand to only gain a marginalized benefit or worse, we lose the opportunity altogether. The Bible teaches that much of the purpose of mankind was lost simply because our "first parents" did not follow God's order. This was a huge mistake that could only later be rectified by His sincere and perfect LOVE. The order is simple:

> *Love God,*
> *Love Me.*
> *Love You.*

That's it! It is amazing how God takes our failures and creates opportunities to share within precious teachable moments. This order represents the key to enjoying a lifetime of healthy and loving relationships. With it, you will find yourself living "life essential"; that which is needed for you to see your worth along with appreciating the value of others. Love begins with **loving God,** the ultimate personification and Chief Architect of love. Out of the life that learns to express its sincere love for God, flows the ability to **love one's self,** the most difficult person you will ever meet, but next to God, the most personal. Finally, the order of love culminates with the ability to **love others,** purely and with lasting covenant, knowing that we become the reflection of God as we help others come to know their worth through love. This revelation healed my heart from secret pain and disappointment and even today, I visit that place in my mind where God met me and reassured me that His love never fails if I remain in His order.

Why Does Order Scare Us So Much?

Order is essential to experiencing success in any area of life. It is the foundation of all existence. The Creation account gives us insight into how God used **arrangement, specificity,** and **balance** to reorder a world torn by chaos. He, by the move of the Spirit and the spoken Word, began to rearrange things that lost their initial assignment back into their proper order. The sun, moon and stars belong in the sky. The waters belong in their place. The grass and trees belong in their place. With arrangement, He specifically designated their particular functions in the ecosystem so that each component could function maximally in the created environment. Finally, He created borders and parameters by giving each part of creation a "balancing" partner. Through this equilibrium, purpose and design for every creature can be seen and respected. The sun ruled the day. The moon ruled the night. The rains where in one firmament balanced by the seas in another firmament. All of this spoke of God's profound dedication to order. The earth in its entirety has been upheld by His powerful Word and maintains its created order.

Man, however from the beginning, has always struggled with order. Something innate within us is fueled by the fact that God created us all with freewill; the power to choose our own directions and our own paths. Often, our selected paths conflict with the prescribed order of God.

We all function in our little worlds living lives that represent the sum total of all of our experiences. Our nature is to protect that world from challenge and change; even if our current arrangement is dysfunctional. We learn how to maneuver and call dysfunction normal. When faced with acknowledging that the present order of our lives is the very thing that sustains the dysfunction, we take offence because we view it as a personal failure. We defend the "fort" and ignore the calls for restructure, all in the name of our personal pride.

Often in relationships, people find it difficult to acknowledge that the pain and hurt they experience while attempting to love, is primarily a result of their disorderly decisions and improper actions. We hate to be wrong and will defend our emotions and feelings from anyone who says we cannot have what we feel - even God. We despise order because with it, we must revisit our way of thinking and living and revoke privileges we have prematurely given to others. We'd rather hurt ourselves than make critical adjustments in our hearts that will end the control that others have over us. Rather than be alone we prefer to date people with whom we do not share similar ideals. Women allow men to abuse them in order to have someone to call their "man". Men allow women to manipulate them in order to have a "fine" woman by their sides. As a pastor, I see this all too often. Disorder causes people to rush into bad situations and improper relationships because they feel that this is their only or last opportunity for love. People are so willing to have someone that they breach proper timing and forsake the order necessary to experience total satisfaction and fulfillment. Sadly, the end result is often the same as Genesis 1- their lives are **without form** and **void**.

The Order and the Bump

Imagine a young man with his whole world in front of him. He's excited. He's overwhelmed with emotion. He's finally found his heart's desire and wants to share it with everyone. He is passionate and has so captivated all of those around him, that his personal joy has become corporate celebration. He's walking around boasting about his love like the proud lover that he is. This is such a great day. But then, he and his love come to a place in the road that is unchartered, perhaps untraveled and not as smooth as the beginning of the journey. For surely if it had been, the young man would have taken precautions and made the appropriate adjustments. But who cared about that then? He had finally gotten the object of his affection to come home with him. Then "BOOM!" His joy turned into panic as his desire began to shake and reel under the affects of a pothole he did not see! "Don't let it fall! Don't let it drop! Don't let my love slip away!" I've waited too long for this!" he screamed!

Then in a moment, the panic is stilled by an impenetrable silence. The object of his affection wasn't destroyed, but someone else was irreparably damaged. Someone who was there to celebrate with him was now harmed. Who knew that this young man's lack of preparation would be someone else's destruction?

This is the familiar story of King David's attempt to bring the Ark of God back to his home in Jerusalem. David, a man after God's own heart, had such a love for God that he desired to return the Ark of God's presence back to its rightful place. No one doubted that David's efforts were sincere, however, David, in his excitement, failed to adequately prepare for the journey. He blindly set out on a mission that he was not equipped to fulfill. He did not know the proper way to handle the Ark. His love caused him to act prematurely and ignore the necessity of the order that was required. As a result, the Ark almost tumbled to the ground and a man died while trying to save it. What should have been a time of celebration turned into a day of suffering, loss and death.

> ***...Because we did not consult Him about the***
> ***proper order."***
> ***(I Chronicles 15:13)***

There is a valuable lesson in this particular text as it relates to value of order and following proper patterns. We must properly prepare ourselves for the bumps and potholes in the road of life and love. Passion should never override principle. Oftentimes, we trade our power that determines how we should move forward in love and relationships for the temporal feelings of immediate happiness and gratification. During these times we must stop and sincerely judge ourselves before a misplaced or mistimed emotion lands us in a situation that ultimately hurts someone and leaves onlookers who were using our lives as their example, confused and disappointed. This is why divorce and failed relationships are increasing within the church. We were never taught to follow the order and pattern of bringing forth lasting, loving relationships.

The axiom is true: *When you fail to plan, you plan to fail!* Following the order and being honest with ourselves tells us whether we are ready for love and its many responsibilities or if we are simply experiencing a fleeting feeling that will diminish in a short while. How many of us have attempted to make lifetime decisions that were based on temporary emotional moments? The essence and intent of love are not seasonal. Love is designed to last a lifetime. This is why order is important. Once we allow our hearts to experience love out of order, it's hard to take it back and return it to its place of innocence. Following love's order prepares us and protects us. Let all things, especially love be done decently and in order.

Loving God

He Can't Help Himself

The LORD has appeared of old to me, [saying]:
"Yes, I have loved you with an everlasting love;
Therefore with lovingkindness I have drawn you.
(Jeremiah 31:3)

We cannot properly begin our preparation to both give and experience love without examining its ultimate definition and personification- **GOD**. If we begin our journey in the proper order of love and relationships, we must spend time at this place and allow our minds and spirits to be stretched beyond their normal capacity to see what love and being in love really requires. What you may discover is that we are already part of the greatest love relationship that we will ever experience. If we pay attention, it will benefit us in our efforts to love others and ourselves. God took the lead for every individual throughout eternity who would ever dare to love someone. Although His love is one that could never be duplicated, it gives us a glimpse of the constant principle of love. It reveals to us the unique devotion He reserves for Himself- *agape'* love. The greatest love of choice is daring to overlook faults and never changing despite the conditions that may challenge it. God is love and He loves being in love with you and me.

God's Divine Addiction

I believe God allows His extremely addictive love for us to remain a mystery. Built into this mysterious concept is the idea of a never-ending pursuit to discover the hidden, real meaning of love. In other words, the pursuit of discovering what we do not know draws us into a search to find what we are looking for. We then become one with the mystery.

We come to passionately embrace the moments of "not-knowing" as we sometimes get faint hints of the answers just before they fade away. We are then left to continue on our journey to search again for what we came so close to possessing.

God's love for us is the world's greatest mystery. Is LOVE who He is or what gives? Does He "feel" it like I do or is it more of a decision or determination based upon what He knows beyond what He feels? What does it mean when John 3:16 says that He "so" loved me? How do you quantify "so" and do I have the capacity to love "so"-ly or just "soulishly?" The problem with the question is that it can only be answered with more questions and every day we are given examples of how much He **loves** us. In Himself. Out of Himself. For His Own Pleasure. Because of His Own Identity. He cannot deny Himself. He is comfortable with His love for us. He sees us in His love and cares for us for His name's sake even when our human incapabilities and our own resistance causes us not to display love to Him as we should. We should all echo the words of David; *"Such knowledge is to wonderful for me..."*

The Mandate of the Mystery

This mystery then becomes the basis for preparing ourselves for our own personal encounters with love. The love that God has for us is so etched into His being that He can truly love without risk of personal contradiction or compromise. He is the greatest lover yet His love has never been reciprocated in the manner it was given. He continues to love perfectly because He has no external factors or experiences that alter the truth. He has chosen to love. When you love like this, you can walk in forgiveness and life's disappointments never master you. God put Himself on the line to display the essence of true love. When He loves you, He loves you! He simply can't help Himself.

God will love you straight to hell if that's where you choose to go. He has never hated you but has disapproved of poor decisions you have made that could have tragically altered your life. Nevertheless, He continues to love perfectly because He knows your predetermined destiny; He must love because this love is what draws us closer to Him.

<u>Death for Life</u>

As we further explore this mystery of God we will find that it also encompasses the "death for life" principle.

By this we know love, because He laid down His life for us. (I John 3:16a)

God is so confident in Himself and in the intensity of His love that He died so we could live; knowing that we would never find another like Him with such a great capacity for love. Because of His God-ness, He unselfishly gave His best to us so that we could live in abundance and give our best to Him. In short, God gave, not gave up. Like Him, we never have to give up ourselves to give of our selves. We'll discuss this concept in detail later.

John implies that we have come to know love within the "love element," a *minute* structure that allows love to culminate into ultimate sacrifice. God's example of sending Christ proves how true love gives life to the object of its affection. He gave His son, an intimate part of Him, for us so that we might be snatched from the jaws of certain death. Christ laid down His life for a demonstration of how much we are worth to God. This is the essence of the gospel of Jesus Christ. His love made me worth dying for. Now, for us, His love makes Him with living for. What an awesome mystery! He just can't help Himself! He loves us just that much!

We Owe Him All

● ● ●

Jesus said to him, "You shall love the LORD your
God with all your heart, with all your soul, and
with all your mind." (Matthew 22:37)

The Father's love for us requires a response. It cannot just be a divine concept amazingly acknowledged and theologically described. It requires a very real and personal response. When we stop and take a good look at the person, measure, and cost of God's love we should be moved to adjust our lives. Beyond the reflection of mere gratitude displayed through our praise, giving, worship, or the other things we do in response to His love, we must alter our mentalities. God, who could have owned us as slaves, instead chose to die for us so that we could be a part of His Royal family. He deserves more than we have ever given. Fortunately, we have an opportunity to change. When we really understand His endless love pursuit of us, we can develop as His children and responsibly give back what rightly belongs to Him.

Think about this. God loves us in a mirror. When He sees us, He sees Himself; His image and His likeness. He treats us like He treats Himself. Everything He has done, and will do flows out of what He sees in the mirror. He provides for us as He provides for Himself. He saved us like He would have saved Himself. Out of love and gratitude our response should be to live as the reflection of what He sees in the Mirror. He superimposed His face on ours and called us His own. He deserves nothing less that to have His image reflected in our lives on a daily basis. We owe Him everything.

> *I beseech you therefore, brethren, by the mercies of God, that you present your bodies a living sacrifice, holy, acceptable to God, which is your reasonable service. And do not be conformed to this world, but be transformed by the renewing of your mind, that you may prove what is that good and acceptable and perfect will of God.*
> *(Romans 12:1-2)*

Every facet of our nature has been redeemed to please Him. We have the capacity to fulfill His every desire. We are challenged to develop the mentality that corresponds to the capacity. Part of the pursuit of understanding the mystery of why and how the Father loves us is the passion we display in pouring out our love toward Him. The more I reflect Him, the more He reveals to me. This life game of "Seek and Find", keeps us ever willing to surrender our own agendas and ambitions to please Him who loved us first.

> *We love Him because He first loved us*
> *(I John 4:19)*

I believe that we are never really taught how to properly love God beyond our service in church, thus we qualify our love for Him by the tenets and ideology of our particular religious environments. One environment says, *"You can't do that and really love the Lord!"* Another persuasion says, *"You can do this and love the Lord because He knows your heart!"* Between going back and forth with our own perceptions, the appropriate return of love back to God gets depleted and people only show their love for Him based on the definitions to which they subscribe.

In my own experience, loving God was not taught as devotion but DUTY! There was no flowing of love toward God in our services. It was about being in your place, sinless and sanctified. *Respect the Pastor! Fear God and the Church Mother!* As long as you possessed those attributes, you loved God! The problem with that kind of teaching is that it did not give one the opportunity to express the tender passion that is required for relationship with God. I did not know how to love Him with my whole heart, soul, body and mind. Sure we sang "My body belongs to God!" but I did not know how to love Him with my body, with my flesh man. We bellowed out *"My SOUL loves Jesus, My SOUL..."* but I wasn't sure how to love Him with my mind and emotions.

My religious environment left so many unanswered questions when it came to developing a genuine, authentic love for God. Later, I discovered that these missing answers caused me to fail miserably in the attempts to love myself and others who God would give me an opportunity to express His heart.

One of life's great tragedies involves never being able to reciprocate, with authenticity, genuine love for God. When we develop a sincere love relationship with Him, we tap into the essence of our divine purpose and revive those qualities within ourselves that can mostly identify with Him. To love Him is to know Him. For years I lived my life detached from loving Him although I was active in ministry. I sang. I preached. I praised. But I did not love.

With all my open expressions of love for God, I didn't realize that I was still unfulfilled. It wasn't until I began pursuing Him beyond my religious mindset, that I understood that loving Him was not about what I did for Him. I needed to concentrate on who I was in Him. I owed Him everything yet only gave Him part of me. He is worth more than just my song or my sermon. He is worthy of my thoughts, my dreams, my ambitions and my secret places. He deserves the best of my passion even when I am navigating through times of hurt and pain.

During his time on earth a lawyer sought to test Jesus concerning the greatest commandment. While the test was given to snare Jesus and diminish His credibility, Jesus' words, spoken from what the Jews called the *Shemah (Deuteronomy 6:4)*, reminded the lawyer that the Lord (his) God was ONE. He is total. He is whole. He does not move in contradiction to Himself. In all that He is and all that He does, He uses the totality of Himself to express the whole of His intent toward His people. When He loves, He does it with all of who He is. With this awareness Jesus gave a powerful explanation of our obligation to God.

> *Jesus said to him, "You shall love the LORD your God with all your heart, with all your soul, and with all your mind."*

In other words, as the Father displays His wholeness in being who He is and through what He does, so too should we employ all of who we are in order to express our profound love toward Him. We are called to gather the sum total of who we are and lavish it on the God who has not withheld His bounty from us. We must stop simply giving Him the "pieces and projects" of our lives. Our hearts should be consumed with Him. Our souls should be moved by Him. Our minds should be set on Him.

When we begin to love the Lord like this, He receives the ultimate glory for the price He paid to love us. He doesn't just deserve more from us. He deserves all! This type of love cannot be denominationally legislated or liturgized. It must come from a grateful heart that has received a revelation of His love. The Bible states, *"while we were YET IN SIN, He commended His love toward us..." (See Romans 5:8).* Since we have found His grace, we should set our love toward Him. From this place, pure worship is birthed; a worship that is personal, passionate, and pure.

Daily I Will Worship Thee

● ● ●

Daily I will worship Thee
Lamb of God who died for me
And extended endless mercies
Daily I Will Worship Thee
Daily I Will Worship Thee

As we begin to embrace, to any degree, the mysterious love that the Father has for us, we should be led with our whole hearts to the place of willingness to live a life worthy of this love. As I said previously, He loved us in a mirror. He paid the ultimate price to see His reflection in us. Our mandate now requires that we live as the very reflection of His image that His undying love purchased. We must be compelled to walk unashamed of our yesterday, focused for our today, and excited about our future. Each and every day our passion for Him should grow, from appreciation to achievement. We should love Him so much that we seek to accomplish His will for our lives. This is the ultimate definition of worship- everyday **living I love You!**

Living I Love You

Normally, we do not live with the consciousness that God wants us to live daily as the profound expression of our love for Him. We are not always cognizant that He is watching over us, patiently waiting in line with the millions of other things we have placed on our important agendas, to be loved. God loves us loving Him. He loves it so much that I believe He takes the time to remind us, both subtly and obviously, with every breeze that touches our faces, with every raindrop that falls, with every flower that blooms. I believe He reminds us to give Him love. When the sun peaks out from behind the clouds of an otherwise dreary day, God so marvelously works to stir us to honor Him not just for that moment, but also throughout the entire day.

God loves to be appreciated through our worship. Because the word "worship" is used primarily in church, we tend to utilize it when we arrive at the building or when we feel a "churchy" moment coming upon us. But worship is a life lived in dedication to someone or something else with the perpetual effort of reminding them that they are the primary object of our affection and attention. Worship acknowledges the profound benefit brought to us by that particular person or thing. In an effort to show appreciation, we go out of our way to always posture ourselves to let them know that they make a difference in our lives.

God never forgets the moments we spend in worship with Him. Demonstrating this intimate type of love is one of our greatest privileges. Remembering to intentionally say, "I love you Lord," each day helps our hearts remain pure and our minds focused. We should long for these precious opportunities with Him.

Daily worship enables us to love ourselves and others. Each day dedicated to loving God strengthens all of our relationships. Talking to Him, sharing with Him, listening to Him prepares us to open our hearts in brilliant transparency. With our failures and imperfections, we can still offer Him a worship that He accepts as a cherished gift. To love God and be loved by Him without pretense raises our self-esteem.

He knows all about us and still meets us in the "cool of the evening.

God does not require that we present Him "big things" or gifts as symbols of our love. In contrast, He enjoys the quiet and personal times when we talk with him and relish in His goodness and love. His heart overflows with joy whenever we celebrate those continual glimpses of His kindness with a smile or gentle prayer of thanks. He is not looking for us to swim the English Channel or climb the heights of Mount Everest but longs for the mere acknowledgement that He makes every moment of our lives worth living.

Loving Him set my life in order. It strengthened my focus and kept Him as the center of my joy. There is a beautiful song that I think appropriately reiterates this thought:

> *I may never swim across the deepest sea*
> *And I may never climb across the mountain peak*
> *I think it's crazy to walk a thousand miles for you*
> *But I'll try to live I love You*
> *I'll try to live I love You*
> *- Zackary Kale*

Our daily worship to the Father prepares our hearts to steadfastly continue on this life journey of loving.

Loving Me

Loving the Unlovable

●●●

...Oh wretched man that I am...
(Romans 7:24a)

L earning to love yourself can be one of the greatest
challenges you will ever face. Most of us live with an
incomplete view of who we are and from that place of distor-
tion, we attempt to discover our true identity and worth based
on loose words, critiques and other unfounded assumptions
offered by those who impact our environment. It is especially
true if you have been raised in a household or family structure where the truth about your purpose was never spoken to
you. You feel as if you have no value.

When words of worth and purpose are not spoken during
our formative years, we grow up using our gifts, talents,
and bodies in an attempt to receive appreciation from others
when we should first esteem ourselves.

Many people in relationships live with these voids, hoping
to discover love and identity in the arms of someone who
will give them significance. But all too often, they find themselves in crisis because their significant other is not equipped
to undertake such a task. That person cannot answer questions of identity because only those answers can be found in
God. Concurrently, if proven that both participants lack self

worth, the relationship will likely be a disaster. How is that for driving without a license?

As we move from our formative years to the functioning years, (those years where we are expected to have a measure of confidence to be responsible participants in the world through our own personal decisions and activity) it becomes easier to normalize our dysfunctions and live with the fact that we don't like who we are but feel powerless to change.

For example, if an abused child isn't given an opportunity while growing up to honestly deal with what happened, he is likely to suffer as an adult struggling to prove that he is pure, purposeful and lovable. He might secretly live with the pain and mask it with other attributes ranging from low-self esteem to extreme arrogance. He may also create a separate world for himself and focus on loving someone else with hopes that the person can help him become more worthy to be accepted.

Sometimes It's Easier

Ironically, when we do not love ourselves, we readily believe that we can still offer genuine love to someone else. This mindset gives us a reason to "de-focus" from our many faults and failures. We can give love because we are not privy to all of our lovers' struggles and pains. Their idiosyncrasies are hidden and if there is a disagreement, we can absolve them from almost any offence while imprisoning ourselves in shrouds of unforgiveness.

Giving value to people we love is easy, but when forced to examine who we are, we believe that there is very little to measure. We can declare that someone else is more than a conqueror and walk away from the conversation feeling utterly defeated. We can turn on the charm and encourage even the lowliest friend while feeling completely depleted within ourselves.

Although loving others is sometimes easier, if we continue to do it while ignoring that we must learn how to love ourselves, we set ourselves up to be manipulated by someone who might use our misguided love as a tool to totally strip us of our worth and purpose. In this place, we become subject to someone else's perverted whims and actions.

Growing up, I was very insecure. I never felt like I fit anywhere; from my family to friends at school and even in the church. I was shorter than everybody. I had a higher voice than everybody. I wasn't the overly masculine athletic type. I wasn't hard. I wore glasses from the 4th grade on. I didn't like my body, hated my nose and my teeth were crooked. And to top it off, I was a crybaby and a momma's boy! (Whew!)

My siblings and friends seemed so self-assured in who they were while I labored to find a mere shred of confidence. There were days when I would just come home from school and cry; not because I was teased but because I just didn't like myself. My mother consistently told me that I was special and that God had a different plan for me if I could just "make it through" those tough years. Still within myself, I felt that I was substandard and unlovable. I would just look in the mirror and cry because I saw someone who no one could really love.

As I grew older, I learned how to use my talents and gifts to camouflage the fact that I did not really love myself. Unfortunately, it led me to experience things that left me deeply scarred. Publicly, I exuded confidence but privately I suffered my own personal rejection asking, *"Why didn't God make me like my siblings or my friends?"* I had no idea that my uniqueness would one day bless the world. I just couldn't see what God saw.

Many can identify with my story of a type of insecurity that produces a subtle self-hatred that affects every facet of life. In relationships, we use people and let ourselves be used hoping that one day our twisted viewpoint will be corrected so that we can be free to love ourselves. We constantly live with feelings of condemnation and self-depreciation that could stem from abuse, parental neglect, insensitive remarks made by peers, or simply a body part that looks awkward. Whatever it is, when we do not know how to love and appreciate the "you" that God made, we will find ourselves seeking external affirmation at the risk of jeopardizing our purity and wholeness. This will continue until we accept the love of God and allow this love to teach us how to love ourselves.

The Theology and Necessity of Self Love

Some of us have never been taught the power of discovering "self" from a clear, biblical perspective. Many churches do not believe in "self-discovery" and "self love." Some only teach the congregation to self-sacrifice; to be saved is to deny yourself.

While this teaching is true in certain instances, it can cause tremendous damage if a balanced approach is not presented with learning to love yourself as a requirement for successful relationships. Self-denial in Christian discipleship does not mean that you should give all of yourself and not receive anything in return. In contrast, with proper training, you learn to love God and yourself in such a way that you progress in His plan for you in order to experience successful and abundant living.

So many in the Church struggle with self-worth and identity that it must be addressed in more than its perceived singular form of producing well-disciplined Christians ready for ministry. People should be taught to live with the blessing of who God made them to be, in spite of what they perceive about themselves. We have often dumped people in ministry work who have no clue of how to genuinely love and relate to others because they have no idea how to give to others what they have never had the benefit to receive for themselves.

We cannot expect people to live with the misconception that ministry and loving other people will solve their personal identity crisis. This belief is not biblical and is downright detrimental to the lives of people who need ministry to teach them how to recover from physically, emotionally, mentally, spiritually and relationally inflicted wounds.

> *And the second like it: You shall love your*
> *neighbor as yourself.*
> *(Matthew 22:39)*

In the order of love, we must also give full attention and obedience to the second portion of the command, *"Love the Lord your God with everything you have."* No problem. *"And love your neighbor just like you love yourself."* Huh? What is that supposed to mean? Is Jesus telling us that in the scope of God, loving Him is just like loving ourselves? Absolutely!

To position ourselves for real love, we must understand and follow these instructions. In them, Jesus gives us the key to why many relationships fail. In church we learn to love and care about others more than we love and care about ourselves. To do otherwise is deemed as selfishness. But Jesus teaches that we cannot love another beyond our capacity to love ourselves. When we love ourselves we develop the ability to emulate God in relationships.

Jesus teaches that self-love and discovery are the platforms for healthy relationships. Who we are to ourselves is who we extend to others. God originally created in us a "pure self" that would one day acknowledge Him and find its true purpose; but somewhere on life's journey, we got sidetracked. Here is what often happens.

Over the course of time, this undiscovered, pure self experiences episodes and environments that create and affect an alternate view of God's original plan. This pure self changes into an affected or "tainted self" that is not at all what God intended. It does what it wants and lives how it wants. It gives abuse and takes it. By the time this self realizes that it needs help and deliverance from God, it has been exposed to hurt, pain, breakups, and so many dysfunctional ideals and thought patterns, that in its current state, it cannot be used for its original intent. This self carries out its own will based upon its own experiences. Who we then present to others is certainly not who God predestined us to be.

If self is ever going to be healed and useful, it must have an encounter with God.. God can recreate the pure self and make it ready to do His will. We must first yield our will, partake in God's mysterious love and come into a profound relationship with Him.

To right the wrong view we have of ourselves we must then become transparent in His unconditional love that covers us. Through this love, we will discover the truth about ourselves and become who we were made to be. understanding that we are worth loving because God made us lovable.

This love must first be exercised in a relationship between me and my *"self"* before it can successfully be extended to others. Once we allow God to teach us how to love ourselves beyond our faults, dislikes, and failures, we can become fruitful in relationships. The love of God must be allowed to heal and prepare us to love others and receive from relationships the kind of love we deserve.

> *"If you aren't good at loving yourself, you will have a difficult time loving anyone, since you'll resent the time and energy you give another person that you aren't even giving to yourself."*
> *-Barbara De Angelis*

Getting What You Deserve

●●●

"The minute you settle for less than you deserve,
you get even less than you settled for."
Maureen Dowd

Everything that God gives us in the earth be received through relationships. The quality of the relationship will determine the quality of the resource that is given. The quality of relationships we have will be based on the quality of who we are. In preparing ourselves to experience the joys of relationship, we must set standards for what we will give and accept based upon what we need to fulfill God's ultimate plan for our lives. We cannot be so eager to experience love that we forget our worth. Before we accept people into our lives and give them our love, we must know our worth and see ourselves as **worthy to be treated with respect.** We must not tolerate being taken in a direction that reverses what God has done in us. We've learned to love ourselves and can be alone and content before giving ourselves to the wrong person.

Love and relationships are already a gamble without us stacking the deck against ourselves. If you allow yourself to establish clear boundaries that you do not compromise, you can protect yourself from being used and tainted. Wait for the true love that God will introduce to you when you are ready.

Love Begins With Self-Attainment

Have you ever been in a relationship where you gave and gave and then somewhere between giving and fighting you said to yourself, *"I deserve more than this!"* My question to you is, *"Do you really?"* The people who usually say this cannot, for the life of them, properly quantify or qualify what they think they deserve. When you ask them they say, *"I don't know. I just deserve better than what I'm getting."* But how do you know what better looks or feels like if you have never experienced it?

We have all have been frustrated with being on the short end of the stick as it relates to what we were willing to tolerate in order to somehow **"bump into better."** This happens because we, in self-sacrifice mode, give up our needs and desires in order to make someone else happy.

Love does not begin with self-sacrifice. It begins with self-discovery and attainment. What you have come to discover, accept, and love about yourself gives you a clear understanding of what you are willing to do to accommodate someone else in your life. Once you have taken the time to discover and attain the purpose for your life and the greatness of who you are, you may determine that the relationship you thought you wanted is not worth the sacrifice!

This is another reason why I believe so many marriages, especially Christian marriages, end in divorce. They marry believing that if they sacrifice enough for one another, they will find happiness and their marriage will last. But you cannot sacrifice what you have not properly gained. It is easy to sacrifice when you have nothing, but when you have spent years working to build a prosperous home and establish a solid family; it is difficult to let go.

Unfortunately years later, some couples call it quits because one or even both of them discovers that a profound part of themselves has been suppressed that would have led them into a totally direction (and hence, to a totally different person). Now the person who benefitted from the sacrifice does not understand why all of a sudden their mate isn't happy

The truth is that the giver sacrificed before they knew what they were really giving up. It is important that you spend time getting to know who you are and begin fulfilling your true purpose. For example, if you discover that you are a man who thrives on making new relationships, you shouldn't give that up to be with a woman who wants you **all** to herself. If you are a woman with a career who thrives in business, do not sacrifice your dreams to be with a man who wants you to be a housewife. But instead, take time to discover those things BEFORE you enter into an intimate relationship. This is how you begin the process of getting what you really deserve in life and in love. Enjoy the God ordained season called "alone" in your life. Embrace it and discover what you deserve!

"Take care to get what you like or
you will be forced to like what you get."
George Bernard Shaw

Going It Alone

"Sometimes you have to stand alone to prove that you can still stand." - Anonymous

We are all unique. Our lives have been specifically designed to meet a need in the earth that requires the unique deposit that has been divinely invested in us. No two people on the face of the earth are the same. God has placed within us our own personal "life map" that will lead us into our particular purpose, and ultimately back to Him without void.

When God placed us here on earth, He understood the ramifications of physically placing us in a realm that is seemingly so far from Him. I think that He knew that life and the proper unfolding of our design would require that we, in the midst of so many other attractants, spend time alone with Him. This is a special time where we are not obligated to attend to the intimate personal needs of anyone else, but explore the wonderful journey of getting to know Him and ourselves without distraction. A time to learn to love ourselves, even if our journeys in life have been rough and left us confused and hurt; a place where the only voice we hear and answer to is His. It is a place where we come into our own; a time called single and a place called alone.

Many men and women do not understand that being single is more than the opposite of being married. It is the opportunity to establish your true identity with God, yourself and with others. You have the privilege of accessing and accomplishing the dreams and passions that the Father has placed on the inside of you. It is the time to pamper and reward yourself for personal achievements. It is a time to identify, adjust, and strategize. It is a season purposefully given to you by God to discover yourself in Him and learn to love who you find.

Being Single Is Not A Curse

It is no secret that women feel more uncomfortable with being single than men. This is because our culture obligates the woman to establish her worth by the success or failure of her husband and children. Little girls grow up playing with dolls and planning weddings. They are subliminally taught to dream of the day when their Prince Charming will come. As they grow older, they believe that a spouse and family are the only keys to a happy ending. Women generally squander their time of singleness hoping and wishing that Mr. Right will come and end the horrid curse of being alone.

On the other hand, during their time alone, single men never really focus on preparing themselves to be more than single. Most of them love loosely, auditioning women to see who can best cater to them. These men have dreams but usually they are not about wedding a beautiful princess. Their dreams consist of beautiful women fawning all over them singing songs like EnVogue's version of *"Giving Him Something He Can Feel"* or Destiny Child's *"Cater to You."*

Men do not appropriately use their single time to prepare themselves and mature so that they can freely give a love that covers, protects, and edifies a woman. Most men, saved and unsaved, see singleness as something you maintain for as long as you can. They do not realize that, this is the perfect time to properly align themselves with God in purpose and position so that one day they can make man's ultimate sacrifice - to love a woman like Christ loves the Church.

God has a strategic plan for your single season. Here you learn how to be naked and unashamed. In this place you can confront your fears and insecurities. During this precious time, you learn to trust God as your source and protector realizing that this season is preparing you for something great. Instead of looking for Mr. or Mrs. Right, singleness affords you the opportunity to **become** the Mr. or Mrs. Right. The church has not done due diligence in making the "alone" season feel like an important part of life. We often make single people feel that they should have no life outside of the working for the Lord. The church primarily focuses on teaching about marriage and families while most of the congregation is single. We do occasionally preach that singleness is a gift but we also cultivate an atmosphere that encourages those who are single to hurry up and find someone to marry.

When a couple gets engaged, there is recognition and applause. They are becoming a family. When they get married, the entire church comes together to celebrate. Why? We are affirming their relationship. When they have children, everyone is elated. They have done well by being fruitful and multiplying. But when you are single, there is no applause but instead skepticism. *"Sister Tammy has been single now for 15 years!"* The Church's response? *"Child, something must be wrong with her!"* *"Brother Jerome has been by himself for 20 years!"* The Church's response? *"Crickets chirping...He must be gay!"* No one gives congratulations. No one affirms their journey in the season of singleness. No one applauds that they still have the freedom to discover themselves. No one considers that your singleness is precious and being used by God to greatly establish you for His purpose.

Celebration is being used as a tool to create anxiety within the single people in the church. Here's the basic principle. Everyone one wants to be celebrated. Singles witness that the church only celebrates those who are getting married and having children. As a result, a subtle mentality emerges that if you want to be celebrated, get married and have children. Many singles, especially women, succumb to this pressure and rush into marriage. They only wanted to be celebrated but didn't realize that the "party" would end. Now their lives have changed. They have made a commitment and spoken vows that they are charged to keep. There is a spouse to love honor and cherish, a partner who has expectations and only after the fact do they realize that they are not ready for what marriages brings. We must change this culture within the Church. Being single is not a curse; instead it is the opportunity for God to help chart your course!

Time for More than Just "Church"
Being single is not the same as being incomplete. Neither is it time for you to devote all of who you are to the ministry and take on projects that married people come up with but then don't have time to complete. I know you get frustrated with hearing:

> **"He who is unmarried cares for the things of the Lord—how he may please the Lord." (I Corinthians 7:32)**

Married people often quote that **on behalf** of the singles in the church. Although single people, because of the absence of familial obligations, do have more time to do "ministry," it is not fair to insist that all your time be spent coming to church, singing in the choir, and praying on the intercessory team. The married people who say this probably didn't follow these same instructions when they were single. I know I didn't. When I was single, I worked in ministry and lived a balanced life. I went to church and served there, but I also enjoyed my hobbies and business ventures.

Being saved and single is not just a time to "find your ministry assignment," but it is the opportunity for you to explore who you are and what you like in a godly context. It is time to access some of your personal passions and enjoy that you are **complete in Him (Christ)**. The place of alone gives you the opportunity to learn to love the "you" that God loves and make preparations to give that "you" to the world. Singleness is a time of reflection and resolve from hurts and experiences that do not need to travel with you beyond this season of your life. Don't allow the pressures of others to make you forfeit the godly gift of your time alone. If you move from singleness before time you will regret it for the rest of your life.

"If you are single today, the portion assigned to you for today is singleness. It is God's gift. Singleness ought not to be viewed as a problem, nor marriage as a right. God in His wisdom and love grants either as a gift."
Elisabeth Elliot in Quest for Love

Don't Be Distracted

At this phase in the order of love, I must admonish that you not be distracted with premature glimpses of a relationship. Though we know that God has a plan for your season of aloneness, so does the enemy. He understands that any place where you feel lonely and incomplete makes you vulnerable to deception and manipulation. To prevent this, you must strategize, guard your heart and control your emotions. Practice loving yourself and do not allow your feelings to dictate your decisions. Hold yourself accountable! Love yourself enough to be honest with yourself.

"Now to the unmarried and the widows I say: It is good for them to stay unmarried, as I am. But if they <u>cannot control themselves</u>, they should marry, for it is better to marry than to burn with passion."
(1 Corinthians 7:8-9)

Paul writes that being single is an ultimate sign of your ability to control of your passions. Single is the season where we learn how to discipline our fleshly desires and channel our energies into establishing ourselves for purpose. Don't leave the burning desire for physical intimacy unguarded. If left unchecked, this desire could force you into marriage for all the wrong reasons. Beloved, hear ye the words of wisdom: ***The heat will cool off and when it does, your might be stuck with someone who you wished had burned up in the fire!*** Do not allow the enemy to make you to the fool you said you would never be. Treasure your gift of singleness and allow God to equip you during the next phase of your love journey.

Words to the Ladies from Gwen

The Principle of the Hidden Treasure

*But we have this treasure in earthen vessels that
the excellence of the power may be of God and not
of us.*
(II Corinthians 4:7)

God has invested hidden treasure in each woman. Like the pearl hidden in the shell, this treasure is not immediately visible to you or to others. The things we go through and experience cause this treasure to manifest itself. How many times have we gone through trials and tribulations and at the end, look at ourselves and say, *"I didn't realize I had that in me!"* God built us to enhance any situation. He already knew what we would face and what "treasure" had to be in us to survive any obstacle.

The world looks at women and views things like money, a beautiful figure, and a top-quality education as our treasures. But God built into us intangible treasures such as patience, endurance, a knack for making something out of nothing and a talent for making people feel safe, comforted and secure. You may not have the best physical figure, that attribute is not always the most important. When a woman becomes saved, a special "power" is deposited in her that becomes her treasure.

We have a great ministry of power, a treasure hidden within us. This is not some **lifeless** power, but a **priceless** power that gives us insight into the glory of God. With this power, we can change situations and circumstances and make ours and someone else's life better.

The problem is that we have been conditioned to look at our physical attributes as the "treasure" we bring to a relationship. We spend money we do not have and valuable time trying to make our physical appearance better. We surmise that our outer shell is the best thing we can bring to a relationship. We allow men to judge that we are *"fine"* only if we meet their standard of beauty. Our response to this should be, *"You don't determine the standard of beauty in my life. If I let you determine this, I give over control of who I am. I am fine not just because of my physical appearance, but because of the treasure God has locked inside of me. And if you are too obtuse to realize that, you're not the man for me!"* Sometimes you have to let a man know that your worth has been predetermined and it is his privilege to be able to attempt to access it.

It takes a strong woman to say this, mean it, and live by its consequences. Yes, there are consequences when we refuse to let others define our beauty. We may find ourselves without a lot of male attention. We may have to learn to encourage ourselves in this regard. We may not have the benefit of having someone tell us that we are incredible and fantastic. When we let outside influences determine our "beauty," we become slaves to that person's perception of "beauty." I am not a slave on the market, waiting for a man to peruse my attributes to determine whether or not he wants to purchase me. No, I am someone who already knows her value and because I know my worth, I can **set the boundaries** on how he is going to treat me.

This may sound wonderful but the sad reality is that women, even saved, anointed women of God, do not live this on a day-to-day basis. When we become saved, we bring into our salvation our concepts of ourselves. We do not realize that our minds must be renewed by the Word of God to see the great "treasure" God has invested in us. We let church culture even dictate our "treasure."

When I joined my church years ago, it was a common practice to divide the women of the church into 3 groups: the *"fine"* women, those who were *"so-so"*, and those who were *"dogs."* The women who were considered *"fine"* did not have to work to get male attention. Men were just attracted to them. We can't fault them, because in most cases they were very beautiful women. But it just goes to show you how even in church, there is an underlying mentality that says men are going to look at you physically before they even consider your heart. Because this mentality exists, many women who may not meet certain standards of beauty, but who are beautiful on the inside, will never be considered for that special intimate relationship.

A woman may have a lot to give, but if she is initially snubbed because of her appearance, she will never get a chance to release what she has to offer from within. Even women beautiful get short-changed. While you may receive a lot of attention from men, how much of it is based on the real you, the inner you? Sometimes you even wonder, *"Does he like me for me or does he like me because of the way I look?"*

Ladies, Let's Get It Together

You must get a revelation from God about the treasure He has hidden inside of you. You must ask Him to make this treasure real to you; to let it be something that permeates your spirit. This is not something you can just put into practice by yourself. It has to be a Word of truth that is nurtured in your spirit. When you know the treasure inside of you, you bring a lot to the table in a relationship. And because you bring a profound portion to the table, you cannot and will not be treated with disrespect. Many of us have been hurt because we felt we had to settle.

> *"Nobody else seems to want me so I need to accept this. I know I'm being treated in a bad way. He only calls me when he wants something. He doesn't take my feelings into account. I don't feel cherished or loved. But it's okay because at least I have someone. At least **someone** wants me."*

When you know who you are and what treasure lies within, you take on a **"God-confidence"** about yourself. This is reflected in your dress, your posture, and your conversation. You carry yourself differently. You understand that you are a gift, a wealth of love, warmth, and grace. No matter what your physical stature looks like, you are attractive to others because you are attractive to yourself.

When you lack this "God-confidence" you open yourself to experience the negative in relationships. For example, so much of the abuse that many women experience in love relationships stems from a poor self-view. We are anointed. We minister to many people but deep down inside we wonder *"What's wrong with me?"* Many times we go through a lot of unnecessary changes because we don't feel good about ourselves as women. This poor self-view is hidden beneath a self that uses activity to conceal it; the person we feel that we *must* be in front of other people.

It is funny how under the anointing you feel like you can conquer the world and know that God has given you this *"mighty thing."* But after the anointing lifts, you are left to deal with how you look at and feel about yourself. God is calling for us to hear Him, to listen carefully to His voice.

His voice that tells us that we are an exceptional treasure, a priceless gift that demands to be opened only by someone who will cherish its contents.

> *I will praise You, for I am fearfully [and] wonder-*
> *fully made; Marvelous are Your works, And [that]*
> *my soul knows very well.*
> *(Psalm 139:14)*

The questions we must ask ourselves are *"Am I ready to take a stand as a woman who knows who she is? Am I ready to be real with myself and deal with those areas where I have allowed others' opinion about my beauty to permeate my spirit? Do I dare carry myself in such a way that says that I am confident in what God has made me to be?"* Don't fool yourself. You will intimidate many men. But often, a strange thing happens when you no longer need the affirmation of men: YOU BECOME ATTRACTIVE TO THEM! When you allow yourself to become the total woman that God has handcrafted,, you exude femininity.

Men will look at you and not really know what it is that attracts them to you. There will just be an intangible something that draws them. When you have allowed yourself to openly display the fullness of the "treasure of womanhood," you are a beautiful thing. When you enter the room, there is that special *something* that lingers like a sweet fragrance in the air. It leaves people asking, *"Who is that?"* Men will no longer approach you casually. They understand that if they approach **this** woman, they must come correct. They understand that you are not a plaything. You are something special; a treasure to be cherished and treated with the utmost respect.

Loving You

When U Becomes Us

●●●

Allowing the heart to love someone is profound. Loving is the personal choice to invite someone else to walk with you on your private journey. Before love comes, your perspectives are yours. Your perceptions are your own private realities. Before loving, you have no intimate challenge to your fortress of life. Until then, you have remained "captain of the mountain" with no risk of being overthrown. Now watch how love changes all of that!

Love In All Its Many Colors

When love is ready to reveal itself between two people, it is vital that they take the time to understand that there are levels of relationships and that love, like Crayola, comes in a *variety of colors*. Love takes on the color of *family*, exemplifying a devotion and dedication to those who God has chosen through a biological or adopted relationship to accept and nurture us. Love takes on the color of *friendship*, those who we meet and connect with for companionship, networking and accountability. Friends can come for a season or they can remain for a lifetime.

Love also comes in the shade of *intimate relationships;* the kinds of relationship where we expose our total selves in order to pursue and achieve marriage, united purpose and procreation. We release affection within this portion of the spectrum desiring to blend our independent identity with another person, so that together, we make our own sacred shade of love. When you are ready to paint this shade of love, make sure that you have developed a strong relationship with God and yourself. If you do this, you will properly identify the types of love that are appropriate for each of your relationships.

If you are like me, you were never taught to identify which level of love a person should receive in your life. Every girl was not supposed to be a girlfriend or a even a friend for that matter. Every man was not supposed to have the time of day. But in ignorance, we classified them according to what we were feeling and needing at the time. We gave them unlimited and unrestricted access to our hearts and secrets without seeing if they would "clear" the security checks (The Holy Spirit and/or our family) in our lives. We did what we do in any other situation when we blindly and ignorantly moved into it-*WE FELL*!

We have all known love through a variety of experiences, but if we arm ourselves with godly wisdom and intelligent action, we can become ready to share our lives with someone else without regrets, loving and living in happiness.

Loving You the Best Way
I Can

●●●

"You shall love your neighbor as yourself."
(Matthew 22:39)

Getting ready for love means that you are preparing to give your heart to and share your love with someone else. As your love grows, your heart should be open to sharing even your most private thoughts. If you find that there are areas that you don't want exposed, then you are not ready to love completely. Areas you want covered, define places where you are not ready to trust. Where there is no trust, love suffocates. If you aren't ready to trust, then this is not your season to love. But when you are ready to love truly and purely, you will courageously risk exposing yourself to either rejection and pain or the blessed reward of returned love and acceptance. Do not fear, finding the right love is worth the gamble.

Getting Ready To Love Beyond Yourself
Real love emanates blessing and favor. When released into our lives, we are happy and fulfilled. It makes us giddy and daring, tender and kind. We feel empowered to take on the world and very little can change our optimistic outlook.

71

The heart holds the key to building lasting relationships on every level. Once we find the right person to love, we can freely express our hearts and minds to them. Our hearts are the witnesses to our worlds, our experiences, issues, fears, desires and expectations. When healthy, the heart is transparent and hopeful, but when wounded, it yields to desperation, despair and even death. This is why we must guard our hearts with all diligence. Protect it from contamination. Padlock it from dream thieves. Pamper it with words of edification. Shield your heart and defend it against predators and abusers. Allowing your heart to be damaged marginalizes your ability to live and love fully.

A secret shared is a trust born.
- a Jedi saying

So many of us learn love by "falling into it," never knowing the care and preparation it takes to establish healthy intimate relationships. If you are like me, you have learned what to do by experiencing what **not** to do. As I shared earlier, I met love in a field across from my uncle's house at age 10. I didn't know anything about it. I didn't know how to explain how I felt. I just "loved." Adults thought that my feelings for this girl were so cute. No one told me to be careful because they did not know how much unreturned love would hurt me even at that age. I dare not try to reduce loving or being in love to an exact science, but never forget that love works best for those who maturely take it step by step.

When Love is Ready

Let's revisit the following text:

"I charge you, O daughters of Jerusalem, by the gazelles or by the does of the field, Do not stir up nor awaken love until it pleases."

72

The New Living Translation states it with clear instruction:

"Promise me, O women of Jerusalem, by the swift gazelles and the deer of the wild, not to awaken love <u>until the time is right</u>. (Emphasis added)

Make this text the foundation of your life as you move forward to develop intimate relationships. The clear message of the text is that if you want the fullness of love and all of its joy, then wait until love stirs or comes of its own accord. In full context, the Shulamite has met her Beloved- the man she has been waiting for all of her life. He comes with what she needs and provides a place for her in his life. They are physically attracted to each other and together they sense the urgency to move into an intimate relationship. But in the midst of all of these intense feelings and emotions, she cautions the daughters of Jerusalem to not engage in love until the right time. In other words, do not be hasty to be in love. Do not force it. Do not give this precious gift to just anyone. True love, because it comes from God, will release itself into your life and bring with it the answers to all of your most intimate questions

Most people "fall" in love because they've move outside of love's timing. Love is not designed to make us fall but to stand taller than we've ever stood before. Many say that love is blind. On the contrary, love causes you to notice things about yourself that you have never seen and it clearly gives you insight into the life of the "someone" of whom you are the complementing piece.

Stop for a minute. Take a breath. Inhale this statement:

"In love, time is my friend."

Now, exhale this one:

**"If I am patient, time will allow love to work for
my good."**

Feel better? If not, you should because you are learning
how not to be influenced by some "internal ticking clock,"
or the undue, unsolicited pressure from family and friends to
find love, get married, have kids, and live happily ever after.
Of course, these are the very same people who are going to
criticize you if you make a mistake. So, allow love to stir
itself up in you by its own appointing.

Too many couples are experiencing the effects of
"making" love happen too soon and spend most of their time
praying for grace to endure seasons of their lives together.
If these couples had been patient allowing love, to have its
perfect work then they would not have experienced the reper-
cussions of misplaced love. Proper delay when beginning to
love can sustain the marriage and stop the divorce.

I cannot count the times when individuals have come
to me in a panicky haste to introduce me to their "significant other." I'm grateful that they seek my approval, but on
every occasion I ask, "Why the rush?" "Is he or she ready
to meet me?" "Are you ready for me to give you my honest
assessment?"

Don't Be "Souled" Into Slavery
Everyone wants to be loved and we all have different
needs that have been left unfulfilled by God. These needs
are connected to our purpose and are touched and met on
various levels by the display of different kinds of love and
care given to us, from family and friends to the intimate relationship between man and woman. The order of love begins
with a profound relationship with the Father who has, out of
His immeasurable love for us, prepared our steps to receive

"love deposits" all along our journey. Throughout that divine path, those who God has destined to give us love simply "fit" into the structure of our lives. They did not force or deceive their way into our hearts. We unwittingly give them access to a place that needed their voice, encouragement, insight or touch.

When we experience love and relationships apart from God's order, we learn the wrong ways to both identity and purpose. We allow people access to us by virtue of mere feelings acquired during a moment desperate anxiety and emotional need. The end result is that we develop ties to people and events that affect the fabric of who we are. When we allow ourselves to be intimately connected to people who have no clue and concern about our destiny, they gain the influence to dictate the way we are loved.

No one can love us beyond the capacity in which they have experienced it. No matter how we communicate what we really need, they are unable to give it because they have no reference point for the love we require. And the honest truth is, we do not have to settle. Make a commitment not to allow your moments of desperation to determine your destiny.

Made with Holes By God's Design

And the LORD God said, "It is not good for the
man to be alone. I will make a companion who
will help him."
(Genesis 2:18 - New Living Translation)

I have often heard that singles should not begin a rela-tionship with "half a person"; that only two whole people can forge a successful commitment. Although I understand the premise behind the thought, it is somewhat unrealistic. Personally, I don't think that joining two totally whole people was ever God's intention. Throughout Scripture, God connects flawed and imperfect people. In His wisdom, He connected them because He knew they could bring success and achievement to each other in the scope of His purpose for their lives.

"True love does not come by finding the perfect
person, but by learning to see an imperfect person
perfectly."
-Jason Jordan

Whole as God defines it, means that we have accepted and healed from those experiences in our lives that at one time would have produced within us condemnation, guilt and shame. These experiences could have disabled our pursuit of purpose, but God's hand of protection blocked any permanent damage. To further understand this concept of wholeness, recognize that we are never complete to the point where we are totally independent of the love and nurture of others. God leaves "holes" or measures of incompletion in us with purpose attached to them so that when we meet the "right" person and connect to them, they add the missing components of our destiny. If I am passionate about my purpose, then I will know and choose the person who can understand, connect to, and help me accomplish it.

Sidebar with the Brothers

Let me share this important point with the brothers. When Adam, the first man, awoke to Eve, the first woman, the Bible doesn't mention a word about her physical attributes. We do not know what she looked like. She could have been fat, skinny, dark, light, etc. We are never told that she was physically attractive.

What we do know however is that when Adam saw her, he immediately recognized that she was created for him and declared, "She is **BONE OF MY BONE** and **FLESH OF MY FLESH**." WOW! In other words, Eve touched the very structure of his being and she therefore qualified to clothe and cover him.

So often men are overtaken by a false sense of masculinity that says they need to have the best looking lady on their arm. Unfortunately, acquiring the "best-looking" woman doesn't mean that you have the "trophy."

And they were both naked, the man and his wife,
and were not ashamed.
(Genesis 2:25)

Seeing Beyond the Wrapping Paper

This is why physical attraction, although important, should not be the ultimate qualifier for choosing a mate. Marriage to an attractive person does not keep you from being attracted to other attractive people. Developing real and intimate love requires that you spend time with an individual to understand where you honestly fit in each other's lives. You need to know if each of you has what it takes to help the other accomplish their divine purpose. The questions to ask yourself are, *"What is his or her relationship with God? Am I called to heal the residue of hurt that she has carried? Can I support his dreams and goals? Do I have the capacity to allow her to blossom as a total woman without becoming insecure? Does his family structure correlate to mine?"* When you can answer affirmatively to these questions, you are on the road to experiencing genuine love.

When love is ready, intimacy will lead you to share things about yourself that only you and God know and have loved. Ready love will tell you that this is the person that you can share this with. This individual can handle your void and supply the missing piece. You won't have to give up your true identity to fit into someone else's mold for loving you. Woman, you won't have to alter your appearance to be accepted by the right man. Man, for the right woman, you won't need to trade your God-given sensitivity to exemplify the epitome of ill-defined masculinity. When the right choice comes your way, you can be yourself and be happily in love.

The Dating Dilemma

Every culture has its courtship rituals. Growing up, adults used an old-fashioned term called *"keeping company or courting."* My parents would not allow us to "court" or "visit" the opposite sex until we were at least sixteen years old. Essentially, "courting" meant that a young man could go to a young lady's house and sit and talk to her with her family nearby, often in the next room. The young man could only couch sit for a short while and he had to meet and speak with the girl's parents before he could sit down and talk. Back then, boys didn't blow horns for young ladies to come out to his car and talk and girls required chivalry and respect from their young beaus. Mothers used to say to their daughters, *"Ain't no boys blowin' no horn for you! Ain't no hookers living here!"* My sister hated growing up in a house full of nosey and protective men, but she learned by example that men were to treat her with courtesy and kindness,,. Likewise as boys, we were taught that it is a privilege to spend time with someone's daughter. When you met her parents, you knew right away there was nothing "going down" and you had better not try it! Boy, is my daughter in trouble! But I digress...

What Does the Bible Say?

When it comes to dating, the Bible is silent. In fact, you do not even find the term in the Scriptures. The closest word that we find in the Scriptures is "betrothal." Betrothal in the Jewish culture was a serious, sacred commitment between a man and a woman. It was not a casual relationship. The word "betrothal" clearly expresses the intention of God regarding relationships between men and women. American culture has given a sense of "casualness" to dating and courtship. As the family unit has lost much of its influence, young men and women have had to basically fend for themselves and come up with their own ideas for dating. When I was young, you couldn't talk about courting or dating without getting the scrutiny and consent of the **entire** family. Some of the first questions I was asked were, *"Boy, who your family is?"* *"What your people do?"* *"Why do you like my daughter?"* If I couldn't satisfy that my family was legitimate and that their name was in good standing, I couldn't see their daughter. *"Oh, you Smitty and Lynette son!"* and my personal favorite *"You belong to Bishop Townsend and them!"* I was in like Flynn then!

Even though family influence has declined and men and women have gone into relationships without familial accountability, God still has a standard by which relationships are to be measured.

The Dangers of Casual Dating

There is much debate among Christians over whether dating is acceptable. I believe each person must have his or her own convictions about it. Brothers and sisters, I have strong feelings about this subject. Please allow me to share my thoughts with you.

I have learned through trial and error and numerous mistakes that casual dating is not God's best. My brothers, I believe that when you approach a woman, you know from the beginning whether you want your relationship with her to be platonic or something else. If you approach her as someone wanting a platonic friendship, then make sure your intentions and actions are clear. You two can hang out with mutual friends but don't ask her to dinner or a movie alone. She should never feel any pressure from you. However, if you approach her with the objective of pursuing something beyond friendship, don't expect her to allow you to date her and **ten other women** until you make a decision regarding who you want. This entire process and your immaturity speak volume to women. They read into the approach.

My sisters, like the brothers, you are also responsible for making your desires clear up front. Do not play games with a man's emotions when he is offering a meal and a commitment and you just want to get out of the house. In contrast, if you are looking for a committed relationship, don't date a man who has already told you that he not ready for that. You cannot change his mind.

When the time and opportunity are right, both men and women begin searching for a committed relationship. When you arrive at this place in your life, all casual dating should cease.

Dating Is A Precursor to Something More

Casual dating almost always leads to one of the individuals wanting more. Eventually one of the parties will require more respect and attention. When this happens, exclusivity will be expected. Along with a change in expectations, look forward to these types of questions: *"How can you date me if your attention is divided among other women?" "Why didn't you answer your phone when I called you?" "Where have you been all day? You didn't tell me where you were going!"* It is dangerous to use dating to "sample" prospects as a prescription for momentary loneliness. When you need a good listener, you call Sally or James. When you want to have a good time, you call Shante' or Roger. When you want spiritual support, Monique or Marcus is the on the cell. If you are so busy *"sampling and tasting"*, how will you ever be able to know the **one** who has been sent to satisfy your appetite and quench your thirst?

These are my personal thoughts and I truly believe they are justified. You should pray and ask the Lord to minister to you concerning this matter and then take time to make some decisions, set guidelines for yourself and follow them.

Some of you may be saying, *"Well, if I don't date, how can you get to know the person?"* If you and the person you are interested in are part of the same ministry, then the life of the ministry affords you several opportunities to observe their character and behavior. You should do this **before** revealing your attraction or interest in that person.

Whether the person you are interested in is not part of your ministry or not, observe them in various environments under diverse conditions. Know what you expect from the relationship and set standards based on your expectations. Do not give your heart, your time or your consideration to someone if they do not meet these criteria.

Don't obligate yourself to a dating situation that will eventually lead to nowhere. Take your time. Explore your friendships and stick to your convictions. You are not a "sample." God has made you someone's standard!

My Brother, My Sister, My Spouse….Maybe!

Within the family of God, most people look first for a soul mate instead of walking the journey with God and a true friend. Often times, the best relationships stem from great friendships. When someone is already connected to you through God, it is easier to accept and love him or her when the time is right. Because you both respect God and understand His purpose for each of you, you value one another as our Father values you. This acknowledgement will automatically establish proper limits for the potential relationship as you consider and decide if love has a purpose for the two of you beyond this level.

Often we miss this critical point. Maybe you were only supposed to be brothers and sisters in Christ. Don't get involved in a personal relationship with someone who was sent to only be your friend. Your choir buddy does not have to date you. Your prayer leader was not sent to fall in love with you. Saved people ruin perfectly good friendships by turning them into romantic relationships with no other foundation other than, "We both love the Lord."

With romantic love comes chemistry, a revealed mix and easy formula for the two people who are ordained to be together. It doesn't require a prophetic word to sanction it. It comes when two people spontaneously react to each other, acknowledging a mutual attraction and sharing a common understanding. Now I agree that love can emerge between best friends who find their common interests in ministry at beginning, but there still must be a mutual attraction confirmed by a divine sanction in the hearts of the two individuals. It is natural and doesn't require force.

When I was younger, there were people in church who thought they we ordained by God to be "District Matchmaker," setting up couples because they "looked good together in Jesus' name." The devil is a liar! Do not succumb to the pressure of dating someone simply because they are saved and you both attend the same church. Love may rise between two people who share similar attributes, but allow your own hearts to be connected by the Lord's leading and mutual consent. God just may have the love of your life sitting right next to you in the pew.

Covering: Love's Greatest Honor and Challenge

●●●

*"A man will be as a hiding place from the wind,
and a cover from the tempest, As rivers of water
in a dry place, As the shadow of a great rock in a
weary land."*
(Isaiah 32:2)

Everyone wants to be loved and protected. It is a natural need within us. When someone trusts you as the protector of their heart and purpose, you are in a position of great honor. Although our Heavenly Father is the Chief Protector, He extends this attribute into the relationship between two people as the sure sign of mutual covenant. I believe that covering for those who need security and reassurance is one of love's greatest attributes.

*"And above all things have fervent love for one
another, for love will cover a multitude of sins."*
(I Peter 4:8)

The Blessing of Covering

Covering is given as a gift and a blessing. It should never be forced on anyone. It holds within it, a tremendous responsibility for those who have made commitments to one another. We are told to cover our families. Members of the church are instructed to cover one another in prayer and encouragement. Friends cover each other through mutual accountability. Some type of covering is needed in almost every aspect of our lives.

We must understand covering before we engage in intimacy with another person. The best example of covering demonstrated when two people come together to establish a lasting and loving relationship.

You deserve to be cherished and protected by someone who has a revelation of your worth. Covering suggests that you are ready to know, handle and protect the secret chambers of your lover's heart. You agree to be their hiding place, their fortress from the storm. You accept their flaws and wait patiently as they work through them. As they heal from wounds, you have consented to shield them from criticism, even your own. You agree to never use your lover's confessed mistakes as a means to manipulate them into doing what you want. You console them when they cry all night long and remind them of their strength in the morning. You take all of who they are and merge it with all of who you are. You are responsible for then in strength and in weakness.

I learned the meaning of covering when my wife's father died. Grief had stricken her functionless. She was not able to move beyond that point. I was accustomed to her being vibrant and strong but this devastating moment broke her. She was hurt beyond measure and extremely vulnerable.

We had young children who needed their mother to be whole when she clearly was not. She didn't want to go to church. She only went to work and came home. There were days and nights when she cried so much that I could feel the tears well in my eyes. I felt her pain. I shared her lost as if her were my own.

One night I prayed for guidance in how to help her with her pain. The Lord said, *"Cover her like I cover you. Share her infirmities until I tell you to speak healing. Be her shield and protect her heart from depression as she mourns. Care for your children and love her into wholeness."* That was difficult. Neither one of us was looking for this tragedy to occur during this time in our young marriage. It caught us completely by surprise. But with guidance from the Holy Spirit and prayer, we made it through those hard days and eventually our lives returned to normal. I believe we would not have made it if God had not taught me how to cover her. Years later, she would cover me through the difficult lost of my sister.

All intimate relationships will have unexpected moments of challenge that require the knowledge of how to properly cover your mate. Doing your season of preparation, ask God to teach you how to cover someone's life and heart. Yes, it will be challenging, but it is one of love's greatest honors.

"...And his banner over me was love."
(Song of Solomon 2:4)

Words to the Ladies from Gwen

To the Ladies- It's Your Choice

*"And in life, it is all about choices we make.
And how the direction of our lives comes down to
the choices we choose."*
*Catherine Pulsifer from HONESTY. . . A Core
Value?*

Most single men and women do not respect or understand the concepts of covenant and covering. We also
do not comprehend the power of intimacy and the risk we take
when we allow it to develop without covenant. God intended
for the woman to be covered and in covenant. She was never
to reproduce without the profound benefits of protection and
care. A girl is to grow up in her father's house and her gifts
and talents are reproduced or developed in the context of
that house. Her father covers and protects her and she reproduces under the nurturing protection of the covenant of with
her father. She does not reproduce for any single individual.
Instead, she reproduces for the benefits of the whole family,
again highlighting the importance of covenant.

In the Israeli betrothal custom, the bride price or the
dowry paid to the father of the bride represented payment
for loss of labor. The woman was looked at as a valuable
addition to the family and now that value would be given to

another family. From her father's house, God intended for the woman to go into her husband's house with the new husband now establishing the covenant and providing the covering. The woman would now be free to reproduce because she was protected.

Today, many women live lives filled with continuous hurt because they have never learned that they were not to reproduce in any form without the benefit of proper covenant and covering. Contemporary culture tells women that they have to give something to get something from a man. Women are conditioned to see to the needs of others. We feel like we have to nurture someone. Because we were created to enhance relationships, we are built to bring things of value to the table. We would think twice about sleeping with a man we were not married to, but we think nothing about reproducing emotionally, spiritually, financially, and physically in the lives of men who have no intention of ever being in covenant with us. Truth be told, this behavior is supported by the culture, even the church. Because of this, we see so many hurting and bruised women end up alone and confused because there was no real understanding of covering and covenant.

Intimacy Produces

Listen, my sister. What men and women fail to remember is that intimacy yields reproduction. If you make love to a man and are capable of reproducing, you probably will. The same principle works if you are intimate with a man emotionally or spiritually. Eventually you will begin to reproduce in his life. He will have given you his seed, whether physical, spiritual or emotional. You will take it and begin to nurture it and reproduce.

How does a man give you his seed? Well, we know how it's done physically, but you need know that when you become intimate with a man, he plants within you seeds of himself. His goals, his thoughts, his feelings, his desires (seeds) are all freely released in moments of intimacy. You don't have to sleep with a man to become intimate. For example, you may be on the phone with him and your conversation becomes intense. Perhaps he shares something about his past or he opens up about a desire he has for his future. At that moment a woman incubates that thought or "seed" and begins to nurture it. She will do whatever she can to help his seed grow and eventually become attached to what she has nurtured and produced.

Many women would never consider being physically intimate with a man without the benefits of covenant, but think nothing of spending money, time, talents, and energy on him. Somehow, we don't perceive that this is a part of intimacy. We only realize the depth of the intimacy when the man chooses another and rejection occurs. Suddenly a light comes on and the woman considers how intimate she has really been and remembers all of the dreams she has nurtured for this man. The man never made any promises, so he feels justified in rejecting her. *"I didn't promise you anything, so why are you so mad?"* This man doesn't understand that intimacy occurred in the relationship and out of it, there was something produced. The pain cuts so deep that it is almost like having a child for a man and after birth, he takes that child away. Then to top that, he gives your child to another woman to cherish while you look on empty-handed and from a distance. Often the pain we feel after we've been rejected is not due to the actual rejection, but by the sense of loss that resulted from what we birthed into the relationship.

Girl, Protect Your "Stuff"

Keep your heart with all diligence,
For out of it [spring] the issues of life.
(Proverbs 4:23)

In a nutshell, women must choose to draw the line and set boundaries within relationships in order to guard their hearts. The Bible admonishes us to our guard our hearts with due diligence. Out of the heart flows those precepts that bring us life. When you give someone your heart without a commitment or covenant, you give that person free reign to do whatever he or she wants.

When a friendship with a man becomes more just platonic, the dynamics of the relationship change and the woman must decide to pull away. Once attraction enters the picture, something as simple as a hug becomes emotionally charged. What may have been a casual peck on the cheek becomes a heartfelt kiss. If there is no covenant or commitment at that point, the woman is in danger

So what would I say to single women? Until there is covenant, the man should get nothing. If he has not made his intentions clear, assume nothing. In the order of God, Adam named Eve **BEFORE** she reproduced for him in covenant. If he needs money, point him to a bank. If he needs prayer, refer him to the intercessory prayer group at church. If he needs emotional support, point him to a counselor or the pastor. But do not under any circumstances, allow yourself to become intimate because the moment you do, you risk the chance of reproducing. Now honestly, this would be difficult for most modern day couples, yet I think women of God will have to choose whether to do things according to culture or Scripture. If God has given you a man, then you don't have to "do" anything. He will set his heart and emotions in line first. If a man is godly and has submitted to God's choice for him, he will not allow you (even if you throw it at him) to reproduce in his life without offering you a commitment or a true covering. Sister, it's your choice.

To the Men
You Need Covering, Too!

● ● ●

"Who can find a virtuous wife? for her worth far above rubies. The heart of her husband safely trusts her; so he will have no lack of gain. She does him good and not evil all the days of her life."
(Proverbs 31:10-12)

I believe that society has been unfair to men. In the effort to assert the equality of women, our needs have often been overlooked and ignored. We have been born into a society whose conventional wisdom says that a man is solely a provider. He meets needs. He doesn't really have needs. This line of thinking is erroneous and so many men suffer in silence as a result of it! We endure hurts and pains that go beyond the physical. We have sensitivities that if mishandled, cause us to retreat. We are taught to provide a safe place for those who are in our lives. Oftentimes in providing security for others, we bear the brunt of responsibility making certain that we protect those in our care. But who covers us? Who keeps us safe? Who can we run to when life and experiences seem to overwhelm us?

The truth is that men need covering too. A man is most vulnerable when he opens his heart and shares it with a woman. Unlike a woman, a man does not share his secrets with his buddies. He seldom shares his dreams and his fears with his *"pard'ners."* He keeps his struggles and anxieties to himself. His heart may explode from housing an over abundance of secrets. He would rather die of a heart attack than to have his heart wounded by an untrustworthy woman who not only shares his secrets with others, but also uses these shared treasures against him. If this ever happens to us in a relationship, we will shut down and the decline of the relationship is inevitable.

Samson's Song

"So Delilah said to Samson, "Please tell me what makes you so strong and what it would take to tie you up securely."
(Judges 16:6 New Living Translation)

Most women are not taught to protect and cherish the sensitivities of a man's heart. No one trains a young lady to be sensitive to her brother's feelings. In society and even in the church, there is no course or extensive information given to women on the how to properly cover a man. Women are not instructed on understanding the spirit of a man; his nature, his nuances or his need for nurturing.

Men and women process pain and hurt differently. A woman forgives but she doesn't forget. A man forgets but he doesn't forgive. A man fights with his fist while a woman fights with her words. So when it comes to moments of disagreement, it is natural for a woman to use words against her "opponent," even if those words are secrets shared in a moment of vulnerability. She can promise never to go there when you are sharing with her, but in a time of "point proving," a woman who does not know how to cover her man will do exactly what Delilah did - use her man's precious secrets against him.

Now I don't totally fault Delilah. She did what ordinary women do. It was Samson's responsibility to make certain that she was the right woman for him. A "covering" woman will never beg you to tell her your secrets or weaknesses. She will wait and qualify herself to be trusted. She would rather earn your trust than manipulate you into a false sense of security. She knows that you possess an analytical and skeptical nature, and when you voluntarily share information with her, it is a clear indication of your earnest trust.

Since God gave Samson the precious gift of strength, Samson should have consulted Him to find the woman who would protect his heart and purpose. I believe Samson was captivated by Delilah's looks. Somehow I can't see him with an unattractive woman. Like Samson, many men often trade inner strength for outer beauty. Just because she's pretty doesn't mean she will protect your purpose.

Sex Is NOT a Substitute

As men, we must set up and adhere to certain standards in order to identify the woman who qualifies to be our covering. We should live in the strength of character and be committed to our walk with the Lord so that we have the proper discernment when choosing the woman who will be our mate. We must commit to keeping ourselves pure before the Lord and not engage in premarital sex. **DON'T CLOSE THE BOOK NOW!**

Our body and seed are God-given gifts that are to be shared with the wife we will cover and who will cover us. We also share our masculine nakedness to show her that she has access to all of us. In doing so, we are saying that we are not ashamed to admit we need covering. With the giving of our seed, we proclaim that we trust her with the "birth" of our future.

Sex is a confirmation that she is your covering, NOT a qualifier for her to become your covering. I am certainly not indicting you for your past. I too have failed in this area, but please allow my journey to be your life's lesson. Don't think that the woman who you have sex with before covenant automatically qualifies to be your covering.

I Didn't Want To, But I Did

I never really wanted sex before marriage. Not just because of my church upbringing (even though they NEVER talked about sex at all. They were just hoping we wouldn't *"do it"*), but because I knew as a child that it was something special. I could tell by the way people talked about it, and my friends always bragged about getting *some*, that it was something of great importance. When I got saved, I developed my own self-view about sex and intimacy. I knew that when I got married, I wanted someone who would appreciate the worth of what we were intimately building and that sexual intercourse would be the ultimate prize we would give each other on our wedding night. This prize would affirm that we had learned from each other's lives becoming so interconnected that it could only culminate in the God-ordained ecstasy

I wanted my heart to be covered first. I always knew that my heart was tender. I knew that when I loved, I loved "hard," so I needed someone who would not manipulate my devotion, my insecurities, and my purpose. My past required that when I looked into that person's eyes, I didn't feel like I was being evaluated or measured by their own puritanical views.

Unfortunately before the proper time, I caved in to my maleness and surrendered to the expectations of others and gave away my virginity. It took me a long time to recover from that because I still wanted my virginity to be the measuring stick for my intimate future.

Premature intimacy complicates the divine indicators in the soul that allow you to be in a serious relationship with someone. Once your flesh and souls become intertwined, even without a proper covenant, you are bound in some way to that person. It is difficult to know if a person possesses the proper attributes to cover you when you violate this principle. You have no idea if she is a virtuous woman worthy of your heart's submission or just another "romp in the hay."

Have You Seen Her?

The Scriptures teach that it takes a virtuous woman to cover a man's heart. Virtuous means to be excellent in moral standing; to have character, to be good. This characteristic makes a woman *"wifey"* material. Rubies are rare and precious stones. This suggests that she is different from any other woman. A man must go to great lengths to find her because every woman does not qualify or fit the description. Once she is found, this woman is worth her price. Why? Because her value directly correlates to the fact that her **man can safely trust in her.** She can cover him.

My brothers, this should be the standard by which you choose the woman who will come into your life. Ask yourself, *"Does she have what it takes to protect my heart? Can she support me when I am vulnerable and still respect me as her strong man? Can she effectively speak words of healing to me? Does she make me feel safe enough to unclothe my emotional self? Has she earned the right for me to give my life for her because she spends her time protecting mine? Does she have a prayer life that can reach God on my behalf when I can't pray for myself? Can I trust her advice?"* If any of the answers to these questions is no, then keep it moving. She is not a woman who qualifies to cover you in your purpose.

Brother, Open Up Your Heart

Don't compromise your need to be heard and held because society normally allocates these characteristics to women. Readying yourself for love is not only preparing to give it but also being ready to receive it and be covered by it. We men short-change ourselves in relationships because we do not want to appear "punkish" or soft with the expression of those needs. Often the appropriate display of these attributes aids in making us more of a man.

Do not be afraid of your woman if she completes something in you that you did not know was missing. If you find yourself opening up to her when you are used to hiding how you feel, trust that she will cover you. Talking to her will make you exchange your *"rapping"* for relating. She will be your lady and safe place; your friend who knows what to do exactly at the right moment, not because you asked her or because God "revealed" it to her, but because she was simply made to do it for you.

By nature, she already knows what you like. She makes it easy for you to live and breathe. She is the missing covering of your heart. She instinctively knows your purpose and doesn't have to adjust to you. She just fits. That's the woman you can't live without and the one the church rarely helps you identify. Why? Because in church we must hear a "God said" before anything is legitimate. This stringent mindset quenches the subtle *"knowings"* in those who are discovering their perfect fit. Love's timing will cause that missing rib to call out to you, and like a GPS, it will guide you to the one designated to help you fulfill your life's assignment.

You Don't Have To Miss It

Y ou don't have to miss the one that God has prepared for you. Yes, there may be many favored prospects, but love will awaken itself to direct you to choose the highly favored among them; that person whose words deeply transform you while unlocking new possibilities within. Get ready to wrap yourself in their presence when they are with you and hunger for the time of their arrival when they are away. Prepare to meet God in them.

You don't have to miss the one who instinctively knows what you need when you can't articulate it. The right one anticipates your next move as if they have been given a blueprint to your purpose. Secretly they cover your faults and publically, they celebrate your favor. They know the value of keeping you whole so they invest themselves equally as a earnest token that suffers too if you fail.

You don't have to miss the one who prepares when you're just projecting, ponders when you're not thinking and prays when you're feeling disconnected from purpose. They are the peace that makes problems cease when life carries you into a tumultuous storm. They weather it with you.

You don't have to miss your covering, your committed partner, your covenant keeper, the one you can depend on through it all when the "it" is too hard to define. They give you a canopy of safety and their banner over you is love. They will forgive while they are hurting; support you when the decision is not in their favor and receive you again even if sometimes you've gone too far.

You don't have to miss it; for if you do, you will never forgive yourself. Choose not to be hasty with this portion of heaven. Wait on love, wait for love. It will stir. It will heal. It will confirm itself if you respect it and its timing. It is enough to cover your faults and remove your shame.

Don't force the love designated for you to wander into the arms of another. Don't allow your ark of intimacy to be the blessings of another man's house because you did not abide in the Father's order. Don't settle for something that must be altered to fit, when you can have a garment custom tailored to suit you.

Don't put your purpose on the line just to be with someone. Avoid obligatory relationships. Don't allow a person who fears losing you to keep you bound. You deserve a relationship with the person who sees the favor you bring into their life and spends their days living to repay it.

I encourage you to wait on the Lord and the love that He has prepared for you. Don't sit in anxiety as if your time will never come. Don't settle for the immediate and jeopardize your ultimate. If love is ready, it will be real. And if love is real, it will complete you in ways that you never dreamed. Prepare now. Ready love is worth the wait!!

Printed in the United States
219072BV00003B/1/P